It's Fine I'm Mad

Paul L. Watson

Copyright © [2024] by [Paul L. Watson]

All rights reserved.

No portion of this book may be reproduced in any form without written permission from the publisher or author, except as permitted by U.S. copyright law.

Contents

Introduction	1
Part I: IT'S FINE	3
Part II: I'M MAD	65
PART III: AND MORE...	121
Acknowledgements	144
Also by Paul Watson:	145

Introduction

It's Fine I'm Mad arrives less than a year after it's predecessor, *The World Needs More Poets*. In the months between the two, there was plenty of reflection on friendships and relationships of past and present that defined the content of this project. At times a thank you note, a love letter, and other times, a break-up letter. *It's Fine, I'm Mad* centers around acknowledging, confronting, and making peace with the endless thoughts and emotions experienced in all forms of relationships: whether it's intrapersonal, interpersonal, relationship with society, our culture, and even the world.

PART 1: IT'S FINE

It's fine, you don't like poetry

But I want to be your favorite author
    In a genre you don't even like
    If I make you think twice
    About any word, any stanza
    I've succeeded
    I want to write about you in a way you recognize
    But can't be too sure
    Yet your heart still skips a beat
    Knowing deep down the words you've now heard
    Feel so relatable and familiar
    As if they are all about you

It's Fine, Time Persists

Sometimes that's all there is to it
   time, always fleeting
   never enough, always too little
   Escaping me
   Escaping us
   It's not intentional
   Not always
   But I should be more deliberate
   We should be very deliberate
   Because time waits for no one
   And I don't want to wait on it
   Not for it to be right
   Or convenient
   I want us to persist
   In spite of time

It's Fine, I Write Lies

To protect the ones I love
    I write truths to confess to the one I love
    The ones that are loved
    On behalf of others
    My stories aren't always mine
    Sometimes they are yours
    Other times, it is theirs that I tell
    I hear them screaming silently
    To get the words out
    The powerless feeling
    Of not being heard
    And their truths deprived of a deserved audience
    For their voices are not yet strong enough
    My lies…their truths

It's fine I'm mad

The months in-between
   The weeks…days
   Weekends and weekdays
   You're nowhere to be seen
   Or heard…
   An afterthought
   If that's all I am
   I'd rather not be a thought of yours at all

It's fine, I just don't get it

I'm not worth your time, am I?
    You say you don't have the time
    But you do, don't you?
    I've asked for it
    Planned well in advance
    Or a moment's notice
    Over and over again
    You're always too busy
    But I've seen you make time for others
    Yet months go by
    Years even, if I don't protest
    I try, and I try
    Do you once think
    "Maybe I should reciprocate"
    What are we, if not friends?

What makes me less worthy?
Why are we never a priority?
Do you just indulge our relationship
Out of habit? Out of pity?

It's fine, if we could

Go back to the days
    Where I had your eyes on me
    Your mind on me
    In all the irresponsible
    Free-spirited ways
    Of yesteryear

It's Fine, I Just Miss You

I long for our time together
   It's been too long
   Even when it hasn't been
   That time spent with you
   Makes all the difference
   A quality-of-life improvement
   In your absence
   Days feel like weeks
   Weeks feel like months
   Months feel like lifetimes
   These lifetimes go by
   And I miss you more
   Than I ever should
   Or ever thought I could

It's fine, I just want you

Like no one has experienced you before
    In a way that is unique to us
    Unfamiliar yet comforting
    Then familiar and arousing
    Natural and instinctual
    What a thing to experience
    When we're practically still strangers

It's Fine, I Just Want Resolution

To all my problems
    To all our problems
    I don't seek conflict
    I never want confrontation
    But you're worth it, so I will
    I will fight for us
    Confront my fears and apprehensions
    I will bring us peace
    It is my mission

It's Fine, I Just Want Fun

I don't want to sit around all day
   Without a plan
   Letting a good day pass me by…
   The right person won't let that happen
   As there's never a dull moment
   In the right company
   Let's relish in the kindness of the weather on this day
   Let's hike and catch our breath
   As nature constantly takes it away
   With all its beauty and wonder
   Let's exchange stories
   Of all the meaningful and trivial
   All that sits on our mind
   Let us have a good time
   Binge watching a show
   Constantly pausing for our own commentary

Let's play a game
That leaves us rolling on the floor laughing
Because we are slightly embarrassed
By how much fun we are having
Doing the silliest of things

It's Fine, I'm Too Logical

I know it
    And I think about it constantly
    I wish I could express those raw unfiltered emotions
    That they weren't so processed and filtered
    Pasteurized thoughts that sit with me so long
    Only to be tossed out like spoiled milk
    I'm practicing and working on it
    The empathy
    Being more deliberate
    More expressive
    There is an emotional side to me
    And like you, I would like to see it too

It's fine, I'm curious

About what it's like to be with someone who understands me
    Who accepts me
    Who knows how to adapt with me
    When life intervenes
    With hurdles and obstacles
    What it's like
    To have genuine friendships
    Who are consistent
    Who make it feel effortless
    To be present
    I'm curious about what reciprocation,
    Of affection, attention, and intention, feels like
    About an alternative reality
    Where I am more than surviving
    Where happiness is the norm
    Peace isn't something I'm desperate for

Because I've obtained it

I'm curious

About the lives of strangers

Their thoughts, their joys, their worries

Are they similar to me and mine?

What turns them on, what turns them off?

I'm curious about you

What that would be like

To experience you

...To see you dance

It's fine, I'm just a mess

I don't know where to begin
    If it'll ever end
    I've never felt such rage
    Such cruelty
    Mockery
    Before today
    Such sadness
    And clarity all at once
    I'm a mess and I can change that
    But I'm not brave enough
    Not yet
    It's one step, but a giant one
    I was on top of the world
    But now, I'm afraid of heights
    I'm afraid of falling

It's fine, I was just lost in your eyes

Noticing all the character within you
    The fierceness, the defiance
    The tenderness, the wisdom
    Your eyes tell so many stories
    And I daydream about them all
    Your eyes…
    I see the way you look at me
    When you think I don't notice
    And I can't help but think
    There is so much to us
    So much good and bad
    So much unknown
    So much undiscovered

It's fine, the truth is...

We have a beautiful connection, or...
   We had a beautiful connection?
   What do you think?
   How would you describe it?
   If it ever existed for you the way it does
   ...Did for me

It's Fine, I'm Fine

I keep telling myself that
   I feign indifference
   Hoping it comes to fruition
   And I can be unbothered
   By the empty gestures
   The cruel remarks
   The judgements
   The unfairness
   The hypocrisy
   The hopelessness of it all
   But if you're to ask me
   How am I doing?
   ...I'm fine

It's fine, I just talk too much

A gentle conversation
   Or so I thought
   Things get heated
   Breakdown of communication
   Words are misinterpreted
   Feelings are hurt
   I try to make it better, but
   The more I say
   The worst things get
   The audacity of me
   To suggest such a thing
   When will I learn
   Stop talking
   My words assault your HP
   In this RPG of a life we have

Until it reaches zero
And you are dead to me
Game Over

It's fine, I feel beautiful

Just like the art on the walls in the galleries
    The sculptures in the gardens
    The birds in the trees
    A snow covered mountain in the backdrop
    A pup in the age of innocence
    Fresh pastries in the morning
    A full moon on a clear night
    Like the candid photos of you on my phone

It's Fine, I'm An Art Form

There is so much about myself I don't understand
    And so much more that I am sure of
    The overthinking
    The complexities I create
    Of the simplest of things
    Being me has been an enlightening experience
    It doesn't make any sense
    Yet, if you catch a glimpse
    Don't avert your eyes
    It is spectacular
    It is an art form
    I am an art form

It's fine, you're an art form

There is so much I don't know about you
    Or understand
    But dammit if I do
    There is a story there to tell
    Or a few
    And I'm intrigued
    By a charm, a complexity, a certainty
    Rough around the edges
    But as gorgeous as ever
    It doesn't make sense
    It doesn't have to
    I can't look away
    It is spectacular
    It is an art form
    You are an art form

It's Fine, I Like You

I like how open you are
    How intelligent and experienced
    Your resilience
    I admire it, I admire you
    Your confidence is attractive
    I don't know how much you disguise
    But I know you do hide facets of yourself
    I know better because I know you
    And what I know is you're worth it

It's fine, I'm lost for words

I
    I don't...
    I...I... just...
    I don't know what to say sometimes

It's fine, I'm here with you

Sitting in your presence
   Or oceans apart
   You have my support
   My confidence
   You have my trust
   You have my heart
   I will defy all odds
   To be there for you

It's fine, aging is such a beautiful thing

And you are no exception
    The wrinkles of experience
    The smile lines highlighting your joy
    The knowledge you've accumulated
    Life goes on and life goes off the rails
    Yet you are always on point
    Aging with such grace
    And bold ambition

It's Fine, Amusing Almost

I'm in love with two
    How lucky for me
    To strike gold twice
    In two different places
    In very different ways
    Some would say I'm lucky
    So lucky to find love more than once
    When some never find it
    Others deny it, and let it pass them by
    But to feel such a feeling
    Almost too good to be true...
    Now upon further reflection
    Can it really be called love
    If I still feel quite alone?

It's fine, I choose to forgive

I forgive myself for the times
   I chose myself over anyone else
   In the moments that I did
   The moments that were necessary
   Regardless of if it was right for anyone else

It's Fine, It's On My Bucket List

Kissing your lips
- As they always draw me in
- From your gaze, to smile, to your laugh
- A look so soft
- I want to touch them the only way I know how
- To feel your lips pressed against mine

You have the most beautiful eyes
- At times, with such intensity
- I try to look, to admire
- Without you noticing
- Then I melt
- When your eyes catch mine

Your mind in so enticing

I want to combat it and compliment it all in one
Challenge you the way you challenge me
The defiance, the stubbornness
The wit, the unintended charm
A mind so attractive
Even more so than it's already brilliant surface

You've fooled yet convinced me
That I need your time
To die without experiencing you in any capacity
Feels like an injustice, a disservice, a crime
And I am no criminal

It's Fine, We All Have Scars

Show me your scars
    I want to know them as well as you do
    Show me where the needles have pierced your skin
    Where incisions were once made
    Tell me of the scars on your heart
    Share stories of your heartbreak
    So that my heart may break with yours
    Tell me of your anguish
    No matter how trivial it may seem to you
    I care about your stories
    Your experiences
    You

IT'S FINE, MY WORTH...

Is not tied to your friendships or relationships with others
    It does not make me less, make me more
    Even when I feel inferior or neglected
    Because I know you
    I know your heart
    I know it's not intentional
    It's not personal
    It's not always about me

It's Fine, But Sounds Lonely

Everyone wants to mean something to someone
    Some of us find our someone
    And suddenly, no one else matters
    Anymore
    The bonds we formed
    Vanish
    Made obsolete
    It's like we never existed
    Priorities change, sure
    But neglecting core relationships
    Does that come with ease?
    How do you live like that?
    With your support group of one
    At the expense of the world

It's fine, but there is a sadness to it

If you don't feel comfortable asking for help
    Or want support
    Words of encouragement
    A hug even…
    I thought that's what friends are for…support

It's Fine, I Remember

Looking forward to seeing you everyday
    Or every other day
    Then every other other day
    Then any chance I got
    Without knowing it
    You brought me the simplest of joys
    On our walks
    During our talks
    Even in the silence between us
    When we looked at each other and just knew
    Now there is immeasurable time between us
    A great distance
    Proximity null and void
    Life gets busy
    But I would drop everything
    Just to walk beside you again

It's fine, but I blame you

Or credit you
    You came into my life and shook everything up
    Not peacefully either
    I've never been able to settle since
    I work harder
    Think bigger
    Dream with more clarity
    I'm a different person
    A version of myself I'm proud of
    One that I recognize
    One worth experiencing
    While personal growth takes some of the blame
    You deserve credit as well

It's fine, it doesn't make any sense

And it doesn't have to
    You can't quantify it
    Sure, adding numbers to it
    Does make it something else
    But nothing any more practical
    Not always
    We're all thinking and not doing
    Because life is that way sometimes
    The invisible borders
    The untested boundaries
    The fear of leaving a bad taste in your mouth
    Offending your essence
    But maybe it's worth the risk
    Taking this philosophy of us
    And doing something with it

Bring it to life, give it meaning
And see where that gets us

It's fine, let's waste time

It's ok
    It really is
    You don't have to do it all
    You can't do it all
    Time is limited
    So let's have some fun
    In the moments we take
    Let's indulge in wasting time together

It's fine, I'm trying to figure it out

How much of the problem is me
    It feels like you crave a lifestyle that I don't compliment
    Where we lack compatibility
    Am I asking too much of you?
    Did I set the bar too high
    For you and I?
    Did I push our relationship
    To this do or die predicament?
    I want so much more for us
    Than to just survive

It's Fine, She Said

"I dare you to fall in love with me"
   I said to her, "it's been done, many times over"
   And then I said...
   "I dare you to recognize it for yourself
   My love, my affection, my appreciation
   And then...acknowledge it if you will"
   She said to me,
   "If the music is good
   The dancing is effortless"
   And I said,
   "Our souls on the dance floor together
   The beauty in life with you is endless"

It's Fine, I Want You to Ruin My Life

But don't say *It's All in Vain*
    Give us memories we won't forget
    Experiences only we share
    Lucky you
    We *Bump* to the same rhythm
    I want you to be my *Sunset Lover*
    My *Moonlight Sonata* after hours
    Imagine
    We're *Slow Dancing in the Dark*
    To the *Wind Tempos*
    Our passion so untamed, fluid, *Raging*
    Like an *Aqueous Transmission*
    This is where *Soul meets Body*
    We hold on tight
    Before we ever *Fly Away*

It's fine, but let's stop performing

Let's talk about something real
    Something meaningful
    Tell me what I don't know
    A little more about you
    What do you miss?
    Who do you miss?
    Tell me about your childhood dreams
    Your dreams now
    What scares you?
    What excites you?
    How do you see yourself?
    I want to know your story
    Enough with the small talk
    Let's add color to life with a heart to heart

It's fine, you'll do

I need a friend
   Who takes an interest
   Who shares details
   Because they care
   That I know their life...
   To be open
   Who asks questions
   Because they care
   To know about my life
   No topic is off limits
   We don't have to pry
   We mean something to one another
   And we live like it...
   Intentionally

It's Fine, Just Love Me Already

Let's dance and sing
    Be free and unencumbered
    Laugh 'til our eyes water
    'Til our stomachs hurt
    Let's keep it simple
    And just live
    And love

It's fine, love is easy

I've fallen in and out of love with you a dozen times
    In numerous lifetimes
    And you, with me

It's Fine, It's True

Time hits a bit differently with you
    It passes swiftly when it needs not
    And the moments in-between are painfully slow
    I miss you and I don't know what to do with that feeling
    Which way to go
    I want to be honest
    But not a man possessed
    I protest to see you to end the longing
    But it just resets the clock
    And reminds me more why you in the first place
    I occupy my mind, my time
    But I still grow weary of your absence
    Some say there is better company out there
    But I'm not searching for better
    When I could keep yours forever

It's fine, but let me ask...

How vulnerable do I need to be
    For you to open up to me?
    I know how difficult it can be
    It takes a great deal of trust
    And a willingness of exposing yourself to risk
    A wavering sense of security
    To start letting someone in
    When that has never been your thing
    And where do you begin
    With someone like me
    Who is also bad at letting others in
    But I've done the work
    And I'm not yet done
    And the results are immeasurable
    Yet, how can I keep opening up to you
    Taking that risk

That you understand me
Without judgment
When I share my world with you
If you pull back
If you don't open up to me?

It's fine, take it from me

Someone who really sees you for you
    Not just the reflection you see in a mirror
    You are everything
    Every bit of beautiful as I say you are
    Attractive the way you are
    With a mind so desirable
    And a heart so kind
    A charm that lives without a care
    You are a breath of fresh air

It's fine, you're making the most of it

Every moment, every minute
    Filling your time so deliberately
    With such precision
    Like it's your final day
    In a world that has become so unfamiliar
    Never to return to what we once knew
    But, decidedly still making it yours
    Again and again

It's fine to slow down

You don't share much with me
   So I don't know you
   Not like I used to
   I don't know what's going on in your life
   Or how you really feel about…anything
   But you give the impression of being
   Exhausted, overwhelmed
   Too busy, preoccupied maybe
   My unsolicited advice…
   Do less
   It's ok to slow down
   Not fill every minute of every day
   At the risk of feeling guilt
   Let it be fleeting
   Relax, take a break
   Even when everything on an ever growing list says otherwise

Demand it of yourself
As much as you demand to maximize your time
Just enjoy the moment
While not planning for what comes next
Make time for even the smallest personal moments
Nothing is wasted on finding your joy in caring for yourself
Have a day without a checklist of life to live
And just live for the day
Afford the opportunity to experience boredom
Scratch the surface of mundane
Even if you fail to seize it

It's fine, I don't think I was made for this

I'm not sure anyone is
    But do we lie to ourselves?
    Or maybe some people love it
    Maybe they thrive where I don't
    I struggle with the obligation
    The responsibility of it all
    The sacrifices made
    Every single day
    I don't want this
    The frustration and anger
    The helplessness
    And hopelessness
    Being a broken record
    Feeling like a failure
    Over and over again

But I will succeed at it
Not only that, I will excel
I will give my all
Despite my feelings
And what I've learned about myself
My heart is fully in it
And I will always see it through
Always

It's fine, there's tomorrow

Forget my yesterday
   Your yesterday
   Our yesterday
   Forget the doubts I had
   Whatever fears consumed you
   The commitments we couldn't make
   I'm growing each day
   I'm learning in so many ways
   So many mistakes left to make
   Many regrets left to be had
   But here's to today
   Cheers to the day
   Where I no longer live suppressed
   By my own thoughts
   Here's to tomorrow where anything can happen

It's Fine, I Live Life

Like I'll never see you again
    Not because I don't want to
    But because I want to so much
    I crave the nostalgia of a time that is not now
    A time far less busy
    Less complicated
    Where we can just be as we please
    But the realization occurs
    I lie to myself that I'm just fine
    Not seeing you again
    Because, when concerning you,
    Anything less than
    Everything
    Everywhere
    All the time
    Is a disappointment

It's fine, I dream of you

To experience the closure we never had
    Those conversations we never finished
    The intents we hinted at
    The opportunities we forewent
    Everything we saved for another day
    Taking time for granted
    Like our days weren't numbered

Part II: I'm Mad

I'M MAD, STILL...

You remain a perpetually unsolved mystery to me
    I'm still unfamiliar with your lips
    With your touch
    Your insecurities
    Your opinions
    What you are capable of
    What are you capable of?
    You provoke my mind in a way that no one should
    And yet I allow it
    I even welcome it

I'm Mad, I'm Afraid

I will say the wrong thing
    Many things, many thoughts
    That will scare you away
    Ruin the best of what we could be
    If there was ever the potential for a ceiling
    If I acted on my desires
    How long would it take for the rejection to set in
    Because there is no way you feel the same way
    I censor myself to spare you the embarrassment
    The resentment from a testimony
    With unintended, but predictable consequences

I'M MAD, I DIDN'T CHOOSE TO LOVE YOU

It just happens and it happened
   I know some would disagree
   Say I allowed the opportunity
   But what a life to live!
   Never getting to know someone else
   Not bonding over mutual interest
   Admiring the differences
   Embracing the challenges
   What a life to live!
   Always hiding for fear of connection
   Fear of looking in the right direction
   And actually finding joy in another

I'm Mad About Life

Specifically, I'm mad that I only get one
    One lifetime and I want to spend it with so many people
    Want to experience so many people
    Particularly you
    I want to experience so many things
    Go so many places
    Particularly with you
    But a good portion of life is spent doing everything else
    That time has to be shared with every other aspect of life
    The irony of it
    Doing the mundane, the routine
    Being responsible for so much
    To do what needs to be done
    Over what I really want to do
    All this to ensure a quality life
    As it's all happening at once

One lifetime, no redo

It's now or never...

But I'm stuck doing the dishes

I'M MAD, I'VE GOT MUSES...

But then there's you...
    I could write about you for a lifetime
    And it still wouldn't put a dent in my thoughts about you

I'M MAD, BUT I'LL GET OVER IT

We were friends in the past
    Good ones
    Only time and distance changed
    Or so I thought
    Because people also change
    And rarely for the better
    We trusted and confided in one another
    I shared my words with you
    And you manipulated them
    I shared my world with you
    And you manipulated it
    Because something else changed too
    Your disposition towards me
    Your bandwidth for me
    Did I do something?

My messages left on read
Indefinitely
I know time passes
People grow apart
But if I didn't know better
I'd think none of it was ever real
My existence almost feels fiction
And at best, I was only a convenience
Until I wasn't

I'm Mad Times Have Changed

Remember that life we lived
    So spirited, so quixotic
    Not a care in the world
    Nothing could stop us
    Not even reality
    We just kept on living
    Each day a new beginning
    Free and free
    No conflict
    No consequences
    Let's go back to that
    Let's stop pretending
    Like it has to be any other way

I'M MAD WE'RE LIKE OIL AND WATER

No matter how much we shake things up
    We don't mix
    Values aren't the same
    Boundaries don't look the same
    We define so much differently
    Even have a different philosophy
    Too much I would have to change
    To be suitable for you...and you, me

I'm mad you make me think twice

About everything I've ever done
    Every decision ever made
    Even if it didn't work
    I want different regrets
    Just to experience you
    I wish I knew someone like you was possible
    Before I accepted that this was the best there is

I'M MAD, BUT I'M LEARNING

I've given so much of myself to those who don't reciprocate
    I try again and again
    Thinking I am being a good friend
    To those who would be ok if we became strangers
    They won't let me in
    Stingy with details
    Shallow with answers
    Leaving me to be vulnerable, alone
    Something about that doesn't sit well
    But as stubborn as I am
    I try and try again
    But I'm observing
    And I'm learning
    I've had enough of part-time friends

I'm Mad I've Allowed Others To Ruin Me

To take my peace
    To provoke my soul and draw ire
    I'm mad at myself for being so gullible
    So trusting, without reason
    For having faith in those who don't even believe in themself
    For seeking consistency in those who haven't experienced it
    But…
    I'm glad I've allowed them to ruin me
    For the better
    For those who stick around
    And for those who don't
    For those who make the time
    And for those who don't
    And those who won't
    I've learned how to live with it

I've opened up
Come out of my shell
My safe space is no longer safe
It's real
And real can get messy at times
Confrontational even
But it always leads to growth
I welcome their presence
I embrace their love
The support of my community
The joy that can only be had
From those that have ruined me

I'm Mad For You

The frustration faced almost daily
    They don't understand how hard you work
    How much it hurts when you can't get it all done
    When you try to right someone else's wrong
    But they tell you, you're the one who is wrong
    Even when it doesn't make sense
    And you're never on the fence
    You know with certainty
    That you certainly know the truth
    The truth being...
    I'm mad about you
    I'm mad for you
    I want to fiercely protect you
    From the hurt, the work, the wrongs of this world
    Even though you don't need it
    I love you in a way no one else knows how

Except yourself

In a way so familiar and necessary

I'M MAD YOU ASKED "WHAT AM I?"

Don't you mean, who am I?
   But to ask " what?"
   I am
   The future
   The present
   Depends who you ask
   "What is he?"
   A minority
   A paradox
   A pariah
   A pity
   A father
   A husband
   A friend
   A neighbor

A stranger
A stoic...
There is so much more than what I am
Because of who I am

I'M MAD AT THE AUDACITY...

Of those who think their children have grandchildren for them
    Pressuring and forcing guilt upon their children
    Like there is an obligation to reproduce for their amusement
    For their "legacy"

    Those who think their children owe them something
    For existing, and the years of child-rearing
    When it was their responsibility to begin with

    The audacity of the parents who weren't supportive
    Who were negligent, who were less than they should of been
    Yet expect a "thank you", and to be taken care of by their child
    The parents who think they are the reason for the success of their child today
    When in fact, it was despite them, not because of them

The audacity of them to be so out of touch with the reality they created
   The burdens they've transferred
   The hardships they've expedited
   The scars they've ensured

I'M MAD SOME IDEAS DON'T DIE

I've tried countless times
    But the idea of you doesn't die
    I think about you all day
    Dream about you all night
    I've hired assassins of thoughts
    And you make them appear amateur
    I think I've moved on
    And you draw me back in
    I try to find every reason to forget you
    And then you give me every reason not to
    I try to pull back
    But your presence is so prevalent
    You have your own gravity
    Always pulling me in
    I'm orbiting you

Every now and then getting so close

Giving me hope

But always at an arm's length

I try to remain mad

But I only remain madly in love with you

I'M MAD YOU COULD SUGGEST

That any friendship of mine is superfluous
    What do you know about it?
    To trivialize, to suggest
    You understand the value of my bond with someone else
    What do you know of meaningful bonds?
    Nothing I presume
    If you would dismiss one so recklessly
    To prove your love to another
    When the only thing it proves
    Is how fallible we are

I'M MADLY...

In love with you
  In a life full of lies
  That much is true

I'M MAD I WASTED SO MUCH TIME...

I cared so much what you thought about me
   When you never thought about me at all

I'm Mad You've Told Me the Truth

Some hard truths
    That hurt to hear at the time
    But I do appreciate it so
    It has been a catalyst to much needed growth
    Personal growth
    Growth in relationships
    An evolved approach to life
    Truths that forced reflection
    And a realignment of values
    Change is hard
    Yet not impossible
    Not always desired
    But sometimes necessary
    The truth, your truth
    Has sparked my enlightenment

I'm Mad, Something is Awry

You treat everything I say with skepticism
   I'm certain you don't trust me
   My words, my actions, my intentions
   But you still follow me down this path
   I would say I admire your bravery
   But concerning you, I am also afraid for me
   I can't explain it, but I know one thing
   It's such a dangerous game you play
   And I don't know the rules

I'M MAD I'VE SPENT SO MUCH ENERGY

Being everyone else
    Not knowing myself
    Not trying to get to know myself
    For years at a time
    Emulating others I thought were more
    Who I thought were better than me
    But how could that be
    If I didn't even know me?
    Lost in the process of fitting in
    Just to stand out enough to be noticed
    By anyone who cared enough to
    I feared too
    The risk of being out of the orbit
    Of those I admired the most
    Those I looked up to

Even if they didn't look at me at all

I'm Mad I Spent So Much Time Fighting

So many battles I didn't have to
    In wars that have long ended
    I could have set my pride aside
    Let my ego go and be humble
    My life is mine
    I wish you understood
    But I don't need you to
    My truth is my truth
    And truth is, I don't need you

I'M MAD I FEEL THIS WAY

I've never felt it before
    Not like this
    So out of control
    So hopelessly in love with you
    The idea of you
    The potential of you
    When you're not mine
    No longer mine
    Never were mine
    I live in my mind
    Where I can be with you
    Where it all makes sense
    Where I'm in control of my own destiny
    Not at the mercy of reality

I'M MAD THIS SONG

Resonates so much
    The pain, the sadness
    The orchestral melody
    Speaks to my trauma
    My fears, my ambitious hypotheticals
    The longing for more
    These lyrics speak to it all
    My heart sinks
    My eyes swell
    And my soul...
    Has never felt more alive

I'M MAD AT MYSELF, BUT I'M TRYING...

I want to be gentler
    Kinder
    For you
    To you
    I love you so much more
    Than before
    But it gets harder to show it
    With so many hardships
    But I want to
    So please, show me how
    To love you the right way
    To touch you and make you feel alive
    Show me the kindness you deserve
    Help me learn to forgive as you do
    Allow me to match your compassion

And make you feel the way you make me feel

I'M MAD YOU TREATED ME LIKE THE DEVIL

When you would put him to shame...
   You never liked me
   Because of where I was from
   Who I was
   What I was
   I had a voice you did not like
   One that embodies autonomy
   I did not simply bow down to you
   I was always kind and respectful
   But that wasn't good enough
   You wanted subservient
   You were a monster I never knew existed
   A hypocrite to your own beliefs
   You tried to make me a pariah
   You failed and you hate me for it

With such a hideous grotesque soul
I've met and conquered demons far kinder than you

I'M MAD, YOU USED TO BE

A more interesting person
   What happened?
   Have I outgrown you?
   Have you grown tired of me?
   You no longer talk about your interests
   Do you no longer have time for them?
   Do you no longer have time for me?
   I ponder which one it is
   If either
   The books you read
   Were always a topic of interest
   Now all those stories are gone
   From flame to ash
   Like the Great Library of Alexandria
   We shared music through the eras
   But now your tune has changed

Challenged each other
But always for the better
Gone are the days of building bonds
Strengthening ties
Letting me in the way I let you in
Maybe you're completely unaware
Maybe you think I no longer care
Or you no longer care that I care
All this to say
I miss who you used to be
Who we used to be

I'M MAD YOU GHOSTED ME

We met because you wanted to
    Waiting around for an encounter
    I was apprehensive at first
    Strangers are not my forte
    But I let kindness shine that day
    And so we met
    And met again and again
    We couldn't help but to know one another
    Even if we didn't want to
    But you did and I did too
    You said you were named after a poet
    I told you, I am a poet
    Writing a book
    And one day you'd be in it
    But I never imagined like this…
    Shame on you for ghosting me

There you go, for whatever reason
You were there until you weren't
What changed? What happened?
What did I miss?
You were there
Friendly for a year
And then without a care
Up and vanished without a word
I didn't have a say
Didn't know what to make of it
Was it proximity?
Was it a new partner?
Was it anything at all?
Was it something I said
God forbid, it's worse
Not that I would know
Because, I just don't know
My mind goes to some places
When I no longer see faces
No voices, no texts
So what's really left?
You are a ghost to me
Because you ghosted me
And here in my thoughts
I am haunted endlessly

I'm Mad I Left Them Behind

I was young
   I had little say in the matter
   But as life goes on
   I reflect with regret on the matter
   The friends left behind
   Childhood legends
   I could have tried
   I could have done better
   But isn't this what happens?
   Life…
   It goes on, and off the rails
   We move on
   We grow together or grow apart
   Proximity the glue
   But now we live too far

I feel like I escaped a bad situation
And never looked back
But I've looked back
For decades
Wishing I, at the least
Said goodbye

I'm Mad At The Missed Opportunities

Because I was too shy
   Or too afraid
   Too awkward
   Too mature
   Rather than living for the moments
   I lived with regret
   But I'm not mad at the regret
   It lets me know
   That there are experiences to be had
   Something more to live for
   If I allow myself to live a little
   Some people wish they were more
   I wish I were less
   Less shy
   Less awkward

Less apprehensive
So that I could live more
And only miss the opportunities
Not intended for me

I'M MAD AT THIS DECISION

I thought twice about everything I could do wrong
    And then I doubled down
    I thought some more
    And triple dipped
    It felt right in my mind at the time
    You were on my mind at the right time

I'M MAD YOU WERE SO GOOD AT IT

Always making me feel out of season
    Always the fool compromising for you
    Giving so much of myself
    To get so little of you in return

I'M MAD THE DAY ARRIVED

I told you the day would come
   That I stop trying
   Because you've made it clear
   That you've stopped trying first
   With more actions than words
   Despite our lengthy conversations
   About the nature of relationships
   I've been accommodating
   Flexible
   Amending even
   And now
   Despite losing all there is
   Everything to admire and love about you
   I'm at peace
   Letting it all go
   No longer concerned about your world

Or fitting into it

I'M MAD I HAVE SO MUCH TO BE MAD ABOUT Pt. 1

Worrying about who accepts me for me
    Who rejects me for me
    Rather than assuming
    What they think they know
    Without getting to know me
    I'm mad I have to worry about being misinterpreted
    That I have to choose my words so carefully
    So calculated it's no longer organic
    I'm mad that I have to work so hard to succeed
    When it's second nature to some of my peers
    And almost a birthright of others
    Mad that it's now so hard to get your attention
    When I once had it with ease
    Out of respect and mutual admiration
    Mad that I constantly have to ask for love

As opposed to the norm, receiving it out of obligation

I'M MAD I HAVE SO MUCH TO BE MAD ABOUT Pt. 2

I'm mad religion has been weaponized to force assimilation
    The death of separation of church and state isn't rebuked
    And politics and politicians feign interest in equality and fairness
    With no altruistic desire to represent the will of the people
    I'm mad healthcare is for profit
    That patients are seen as customers
    That society treats what ails us rather than prevent it
    I'm mad that truth and fact are now subjective
    And that quality and accurate education is trivialized
    That history can be rewritten or omitted to coddle weak-minded individuals
    Who fear to live in a world in which they are actively creating
    I'm mad my child has to grow up in a world such as this one
    When I once thought the future would be so much better for him

PART III: AND MORE...

I'M MOURNING

The loss of tacos on Tuesdays with you
    Mid-week escapades
    Gone are the days
    Helping each other find our way
    The life and death of me
    The end of consistency
    I've spent lifetimes
    Seeking the right company
    And you felt right for me
    But I got too comfortable
    With you here right in front of me
    And now we're so distant and empty
    We fake it, like nothing has changed
    But I mourn us every day
    Knowing nothing is the same

I'M ASKING THAT YOU...

Give me your presence
    Don't just be present with your mind elsewhere
    Tired and exhausted
    Depleted even
    Just going through the motions
    Putting on a performance
    A projection
    Of what you think I want
    Nothing real to give in the moment
    Get your rest
    And let's try this again

I'M SEEING GHOSTS FROM THE PAST

Her resemblance was uncanny to yours
   I had to do a double take
   And questioned if I could trust my eyes
   Did I see what was in front of me
   Or did I see what I hoped to see
   Who I hoped to see
   But I couldn't be sure enough to say anything
   But now my mind is flooded with memories of you
   Moments
   Experiences
   I dreamt of us catching up
   Like old times
   Meeting the person you've become
   ...
   I saw him, or so I thought

My old friend

Like brothers we were

But it was someone else

Just the personification of him

In someone else

It was comforting and unsettling

To connect with someone new

Because they remind me so much of someone else

A bit surreal, a reminder of the past

A revival, but not the same

Because in reality, ghosts usually remain that way

I'm hopeful to win...

Your virtue
   Your wisdom
   Your heart
   To benefit from all that you are
   So that you may complement all that I am not

I'm Conflicted, Confused Even

You care about me
    But you don't act like it
    In my absence, you worry
    You seem to actually miss me
    But you would never say it
    And when I'm present, you're absent
    You're distant
    Disinterested
    But, not really?
    It's hard to tell
    There's little I know of these things
    But I do know
    It's not up to me to maintain friendships
    It's up to us

I'M DISILLUSIONED BY YOU

By what I thought you were
    By what fantastical ideas of you I had
    I thought there was more than the emptiness you showed
    But, seemingly a minimalist in more ways than one
    I thought there was more color to you
    Than the bland palette you idealize
    More adventure than this conservative lifestyle
    I used to think you and I were special
    That our conversations were different
    Our bond, different
    Much deeper than surface level
    Unique and intimate
    But now it seems to be more clear than ever
    With so many conditions
    So many excuses
    You're no different from the rest

Nothing separates me from the rest
If anything, it's that I get less
Why did I ever think otherwise?
Maybe I was projecting
Maybe it was wishful thinking
But now I can see the truth
There is nothing special about you

I'm perplexed, you are...

Wildly inconsistent with me
    Yet I can't get enough
    I can't let go of what I know I should
    All it takes is the bare minimum
    And I'm baited and reeled back in

I'm Enamored By The Vulgarity Of It All

Life imitating art
    Art a reflection of life
    The female anatomy offending
    The mind of a woman terrifying insecure men
    Just by existing
    Each one a goddess amongst us
    That should be revered
    Respected and protected
    But we're ruled by cowards
    Trying to tame beings far beyond comprehension

I'm curious...

Did you ever want to be loved and loved in return?
    Or did you want someone to share your life with?
    Or just someone to live with to not be alone indefinitely?
    Because you don't like to be alone?
    Someone to make life a little easier
    Make ends meet
    Did you do it because that's what everyone else does
    Tradition, it's the thing to do
    And I'm curious still
    Why are you so averse to feelings
    Positive ones
    Compliments
    Romantic ones
    Isn't that what this is all about?
    Love?
    My curiosity for you keeps me alive for now

Yet, I know I'll die uninformed, unsatisfied

I'm Sorry, I Can't Help Myself

I want you
   I want your tomorrow
   Starting today
   I want in
   To go all in
   And that may complicate things
   But I want to hear you sing
   I want to see you swim
   I want to feel the warmth of you letting me in
   Become familiar with the scent and touch of your skin
   I want in
   Your heart and mind
   I think now is the time
   Even if it makes a mess of things

I'm Stubborn, Or Is It Something Else?

Maybe I'm persistent
   Or defiant
   Resilient maybe?
   Determined
   Obsessed?...no, not that
   Maximizing opportunity?
   Taking advantage of life while it's worth living
   With those who are
   Creating moments
   Testing the waters
   To see what's tangible
   Or maybe I am just consistent
   I will try and try
   If you're worth it

I'VE BEEN THINKING

I don't want to trivialize the present we live in
   But we can do so much better
   We can do so much differently

I'VE BEEN DREAMING

So I ask myself
    Can I fall in love with you through my dreams alone?
    You've been on my mind, in my home
    It always feels so real until it isn't
    It takes a long time to recover
    From that reality check
    Waking up
    Knowing
    That this was never real
    And can't be
    Until I dream again
    I spend all day awaiting the hour my eyes shut
    And the sandman goes to work
    Taking me to a place where you're real all over again

I'M BAD WITH RULES

This world likes to play games
    With its rules and rule breaking
    Those rule-breakers
    Of which I am one
    When it counts the most
    I trust no one has my best interest besides me
    So I play by my own rules
    Or I want to
    I want to win
    And win big
    I've spent too much time waiting and waiting
    For my turn as I let everyone else by
    ...I'm done waiting

It's me, I'm me...

I am everything I know
    It all begins with me
    Marble runs and magnet tiles
    My life is a maze
    I'm either going this way or that way
    Always feeling lost
    Being pulled any given direction
    By an invisible force
    I'm all too familiar with...
    Me, my ego, my conscience

I'm sorry, life made me realize

I don't want more children
    Though there are fleeting moments
    Where I do, for you...
    I've learned how selfish I am
    Not to say that I am truly selfish
    But that I care more about my needs than I once thought
    I've learned how much my personal time matters to me
    How much people matter to me
    My time with friends
    And most importantly, my time with you...
    My freedoms, my flexibility
    The financial responsibility
    Maybe it's an adverse reaction to more responsibility
    But I also don't want your suffering
    The unknowns with any pregnancy

The known hardships

The unpredictability and the foreseeable

I'm risk averse

I think about the environmental impact

Financial, mental, physical impact

This political climate

I don't want another child to weather that storm

I want to give the best of me

My time, my energy

To the son I already have

And knowing what I know

And what I don't...

I just can't, I won't

I'M THINKING THAT I WILL

Look back on these days
   And be filled with fondness and nostalgia
   Of the youth and energy
   That once existed
   The ease in which some things came
   And the regret of not making the most of it
   The notion that I could've done things better
   Or at least differently for a better outcome
   I could've tried harder
   To have the foresight to know
   that in hindsight
   I will feel this way
   But do little to change it
   Because in this moment
   I lack the experience
   To put my own premonition to us

It's Ok, No Thanks Necessary

I give you gifts with no expectations
    No need for an occasion
    It's my way of thanking you
    Showing you my appreciation
    For gifting me
    Endless inspiration
    Motivation
    Validation
    For all of the above
    And everything unmentioned
    Today I gift you my art
    My words
    And I thank you

Acknowledgements

We did it again! I say we because it takes a community of people for me to pull inspiration from and receive motivation and support to write a second book. Thank you friends, family, acquaintances, and strangers alike, from deep bonds to chance encounters, all the experiences had within these groups had inspired the writing in this book. A special thank you to the inevitable muse who was the catalyst to this entire project.

Also by Paul Watson:

The World Needs More Poets

Milton Keynes UK
Ingram Content Group UK Ltd.
UKHW040055031224
451863UK00004B/278